JUNGLE TREK

Story by Dianne Wolfer
Illustrations by Mark Wilson

NELSON
CENGAGE Learning™

Jungle Trek

Text: Dianne Wolfer
Illustrations: Mark Wilson
Editor: Angelique Campbell-Muir
Design: Leigh Ashforth

PM Extras Chapter Books
Sapphire Level 29 Set A
The Bommyknocker Tree
The Man Who Measured the World
Eric's Thai Travel Diary
H for Horrible
Jungle Trek
Lizard Tongue

Text © 2004 Dianne Wolfer
Illustrations © 2004 Cengage Learning Australia Pty Limited

ISBN 978 0 17 011711 1
ISBN 978 0 17 011709 8 (set)

Cengage Learning Australia
Level 7, 80 Dorcas Street
South Melbourne, Victoria Australia 3205
Phone: 1300 790 853

Cengage Learning New Zealand
Unit 4B Rosedale Office Park
331 Rosedale Road, Albany, North Shore NZ 0632
Phone: 0508 635 766

For learning solutions, visit cengage.com.au

Printed in China by 1010 Printing International Ltd
4 5 6 7 8 9 10 12 11 10 09 08

Contents

CHAPTER 1

No Buts!

'But what will we do each day?'

'I told you, David, we'll be hiking. And I'll be taking photos for the magazine. It won't be easy. Some days we'll be walking from dawn till dusk.'

'Do I *have* to go?'

'We've already been through this…'

'Why can't I stay with Grandma?'

'Ten days is too long,' Mum replied. 'You know she hasn't been well.'

'What about Jared's family. They like having me.'

'Not for ten days!'

'But...'

'No buts, David, it's already organised.'

Once Mum gets *that tone* in her voice, there's no point arguing. I slammed the kitchen door and went outside to shoot a few baskets. I knew there was nothing I could do to make her change her mind.

The next day I heard Mum on the telephone confirming our tickets with the travel agent.

'We'll be joining the group in Port Moresby. Yes, two tickets. One for my son and one for me. No, he's twelve. Yes, he's very fit. I'm sure he'll be able to cope...'

'Where's Port Moresby?' I asked Mum after she'd hung up.

'Port Moresby is the capital of Papua New Guinea. We'll stay there overnight before catching a smaller plane into the mountains.'

Mum is a wildlife photographer. She specialises in insects and Papua New Guinea has the best bugs in the world! A nature magazine has commissioned an article on the insects that live along some famous walking trail. Mum will be snapping pictures of butterflies, but there's an endangered beetle she's also hoping to find.

Mum's been planning this trip for months. I was sure that somehow I'd be able to get out of it. Unfortunately that's not looking likely.

'Mum, I spoke to Jared,' I said casually. 'His family isn't doing anything during the holidays. He reckons his dad will need help with hay baling...'

'David, the answer is no! I want us to go together. A mother-and-son adventure. It'll be fun.'

Hiking through muddy, mosquito-infested jungle – I don't think so! I stormed outside again with my basketball.

Bang, bounce, bang. Maybe I can break my hoop record. Bang. It isn't fair! Just because Mum wants to go and take photos, I have to get dragged along.

Bang, bounce. If Dad was alive, I bet he'd let me stay home! Bang, bounce, bang...

CHAPTER 2

Bug Fanatics

Okay, I have to admit, the flight was pretty cool.

They showed a movie and the meals came on little trays with lots of small packets and containers. The flight attendants kept offering me lemonade and juice. But the best thing was flushing the toilet. It sounded supersonic!

By the time we landed in Port Moresby I was *almost* happy that Mum had made me come along. Almost, but not quite.

The tour organiser met us in the arrival hall. What a place!

There were people everywhere, balancing bags of groceries, nursing babies, holding bush knives… and they had the wildest hair! Masses of thick, black frizz, decorated with bright stretchies and hats made from cuscus fur. I flicked my lanky fringe off my face, feeling totally jealous.

A mini-bus whisked us through the dusty streets to our hotel, managing somehow to avoid the dogs and people stepping out in front of us.

The hotel had a pool, so that's where I spent the afternoon. Then, at five o'clock, Mum said I had to go with her to the hike briefing.

There were six others in the group. All bug fanatics! Did I mention that this trek was specially designed for insect enthusiasts? Mum reckons Papua New Guinea has more kinds of insects than any other place in the world. So, not only will we be scrambling through the jungle for ten days, we'll be on a continual bug-hunt. And I'll have to listen to endless conversations about wings and antennae and proboscises and leg segments... Boring!

The other trekkers were all Mum's age, but they seemed okay. After we introduced ourselves, the group leader began talking.

'We'll meet in the lobby at 5.00 a.m. The flight leaves at 6.00 a.m. and we'll need to check-in our food and daypacks,' she said.

'Make sure you keep water, your camera and any other essentials in your daypack. Once we reach Kokoda, we'll meet our porters, visit the museum and then begin trekking. Any questions?'

There were heaps! I sipped my drink and finished writing up the day's events in my journal.

Wednesday, 7.00 p.m.

Just as I suspected. There are no other kids in the group. Looks like I'm in for a boring ten days with bug-obsessed adults. One of the guys seems okay. At least he talked to me, and listened. For all the interest the others showed, I might have been a common dung beetle!

At last, they've stopped talking. My stomach's grumbling. It must be time for dinner...

CHAPTER 3

Too Easy?

The flight over the mountains was amazing.
After waiting for hours at the airstrip, we piled
into this wicked, fifteen-seater aeroplane. I sat
behind the pilot, so I could watch everything he
did. He really knew his stuff. As we came in to
land, we were in total cloud. He banked steeply.
It felt like we were falling through the air. Mum
looked worried, but after a few ear-popping
minutes, we came out below the cloud cover in
time to spiral down, line up with the runway
and land. It was the best flight ever!

We met out porters on the airstrip. Luke was my helper. He's only six years older than me. I felt mean having him carry my gear, but Luke just laughed and told me how much he loved being a porter.

'Not many jobs here,' he said. 'Good pay, fresh air, interesting people. Too easy...'

I watched him lift my backpack and stroll up the first steep hill. Easy, I thought, as sweat poured down my face. Easy, I wondered as I puffed along behind...

Phew! Despite all the hours I'd spent training, this was not easy for me at all.

'How are you going?' Mum asked as we flopped onto a couple of logs for a break.

'Getting there,' I gasped.

'Good on you,' she whispered. 'I'm very proud of you!'

I never know what to say when Mum gets mushy, so I offered her some of my muesli bar.

'No thanks, David. I'm going to see if I can find any butterflies, but you enjoy it.'

The head porter led the adults on a short insect search. As they lifted rotting logs and scratched at the bark of trees I took out my journal.

Thursday – Day 1 of the Hike

It's not too bad so far. Luke is pretty good company. He was telling me about his village. He says we'll reach it in two days. And he says there is a school there. The way he spoke it sounds like that's something unusual!

'David, quick!' It was Mum. I dropped my journal and raced towards her.

'Are you okay?'

'Yes, look! It's a Giant Spiny Stick Insect.'

What? I looked. There they were, six adults oohing and aahing over this long skinny bug. Mum was focusing her camera and clicking madly. In between shots, the group leader measured its length, while Hans, the tall man who had asked me my name, was almost swooning with delight. I looked at Luke and rolled my eyes. We tried not to laugh.

CHAPTER ④

Falling

Friday – Day 2 of the Hike

Luke's really funny. We tell each other jokes. He's smart, too, even though he only went to school until grade four. After that he had to help his dad in the village garden. Luke's been a porter for almost a year now and this is his eleventh trek. He has an amazing bush knife (everyone here has one). He used it to cut a walking stick for me. We'll be at Luke's village tomorrow. He has another bush knife at home. He said I can use it, if it's okay with Mum...

Saturday – Day 3 of the Hike

We're getting into a routine. Up early, hike till lunchtime, have a look around for beetles and butterflies, then hike until evening. My legs don't ache as much and sometimes it's almost fun (not that I'll tell Mum that). I've been spending most of my time with Luke. We walk ahead. That way I can pretend I'm not with the bug maniacs.

'David, can you help me?'

Mum was struggling to wrap a plastic sheet over her daypack. She was worried about the humidity affecting her expensive lenses, and this soaking rain wasn't helping. I tied the edges so that it wouldn't fly off.

'Thanks, David. That's better.'

The group leader called us together. 'This rain has made the track more dangerous than usual,' she said. 'There are two steep downhill sections ahead. We'll be dropping 780 metres in altitude. Please watch every step. Try not to slip, and stay near a buddy.'

I looked at Luke. He grinned. We hoisted our loads and began hiking.

'Did you hear the one about the teacher?' Luke asked. He chuckled. 'This is my sister's favourite joke...'

I smiled and waited for him to continue.

'What did the teacher say when her eye rolled down the hill?'

'I don't know. What?'

'Oh no! There goes another pupil!'

I groaned. 'That's terrible! Okay, now I've got one for you. What did the monster say—'

'Help!'

The sudden cry silenced me. It was Mum! I dropped my daypack and ran back along the path, slipping, sliding and cursing the mud.

CHAPTER 5

Stranded

Mum was lying on the ground, biting her lip and clutching her ankle.

'Mum, are you okay?' She tried to smile, but it turned into a grimace.

'What happened?'

'I fell...'

'Help me take off her boot,' I called to the others.

'Wait,' Hans said. 'I've done some medical training. If your mother has broken her ankle, it may be better to leave the boot on.'

Hans lifted Mum onto a ground sheet and propped her against a log. 'Can you move your foot?' he asked.

Mum gasped in pain as she tried.

'How far is the next village?'

'Another five hours' walk,' the group leader said. Mum's face turned even paler.

'But there is an airstrip there,' she added. 'I'll send someone ahead with a message.' She turned to Mum. 'It will be too late to airlift you out today, but it should be possible in the morning. It will be a long night, but I do have some painkillers.'

'Can you hobble?' I asked.

Mum nodded. 'I'll try.'

Hans and a porter supported Mum's weight and she hopped along as best she could.

Whenever the path was wide enough, I walked beside Mum, telling jokes and stories, trying to keep her mind off the pain. She pretended she was okay, but I could see how much every dip in the track jolted her ankle.

We walked the last two hours in darkness. There was no moon and the steady rain had soaked us through. We reached Luke's village just after 8.00 p.m. A bed was already set up for Mum. She took another painkiller and collapsed into a deep sleep.

Even though I was exhausted it took me ages to get to sleep. Somewhere nearby a dog was howling and the local roosters seemed to be having a contest to decide the midnight squawking champion.

It rained all night.

Hans had had to cut the laces to remove Mum's boot. The good news was that her ankle wasn't broken. But it was a really bad sprain.

We learnt via the crackling radio that there was no chance of a plane landing in the morning. If the mist cleared, though, they'd try to schedule one for the next day.

'We'll have to go on,' the tour guide said. 'There are not enough supplies for us all to stay longer. We'd be a burden on the village.'

'But you can't just leave us,' I said.

'You'll be fine, David.' She handed me a few more painkillers for Mum. 'Luke will stay with you. His father can coordinate the evacuation flight. Don't worry. You're in good hands.

'But…'

'You'll be fine. We'll see you in Port Moresby.'

I watched them walk into the mist and thought that I had never felt so alone.

Mum put her hand on my shoulder. 'I need to sleep,' she said. 'Will you be okay?'

I nodded and took a deep breath.

I sat by Mum's bedside for hours. At some stage I must have dozed off. When I woke up Luke was sitting by the door.

'My grandmother says you need a break.'

'I'm okay.'

Luke waved to someone outside and an old lady stepped in. She had a basin of water.

'This is Oala, my grandmother.' I nodded to her and smiled. 'She wants to know if you have soap?' Luke asked.

'Of course.'

'Soap is expensive in our country,' Luke said, noticing my puzzled expression. 'Grandma wants you to leave so she can wash your mother.'

'Okay,' I said, blushing.

CHAPTER 6

Show and Tell

I followed Luke out of the tent and into the courtyard. The rain had finally stopped, but thick mist still covered the surrounding mountains.

'When do you think it will clear?' I asked.

Luke shrugged. 'Maybe tomorrow. Maybe not.'

'Where is the airstrip?'

'I'll show you.'

We walked to the end of the village. Luke pointed. I stared at the airstrip not believing what I saw. It was on an angle – on the side of a hill!

'You mean planes actually land on that?'

Luke grinned. 'It looks worse than it is. The pilot lands, taxis uphill to the flatter end then turns the plane so it can't roll backwards.'

'And when they take-off again?'

He laughed. 'That's even more exciting. The pilot turns the plane and immediately gains speed. Then there is a bump at the end of the strip that the plane bounces off at the last minute.'

I swallowed.

'Don't worry,' Luke said. 'There have only been two accidents in the past five years...'

I didn't want to know any more. 'Let's see the rest of the village,' I suggested.

'Okay, I'll show you our school.'

We walked through the village square, followed by a mob of dogs and young children. There was a class in session, but the teacher stopped and welcomed us. I looked around. There were three worn-out books on a shelf and the teacher was using a wet cloth to write sums on the blackboard.

'Don't you use chalk?' I asked.

'We ran out last year,' Luke said.

'What about pencils, and paper?'

'There is no money.'

I tried to hide my shock. Then I remembered my journal.

'I have some paper, and pens.'

The kids sat up in excitement.

I ripped up my journal and handed out my pens, pencils and coloured markers. We spent the afternoon writing messages and copying each other's drawings. The teacher seemed thrilled at the interruption to his lesson. He kept shaking my hand and thanking me.

After school the kids took me into the jungle and showed me how to cut vines to weave into baskets. They taught me songs and we played scarecrow tag. Then I suddenly remembered Mum.

'I have to get back,' I said, feeling guilty that I'd forgotten about her for so long.

'Wait,' Luke said. 'There is something I want to show you.'

He led me into the jungle and stopped in front of a small creek. Luke parted some vines then scooped up a beetle. It was huge with a beautiful metallic-looking carapace.

'Is this the one your mother has been looking for?' he asked.

'Yes, I think so,' I cried with bug-fanatic excitement. 'It is a rhinoceros beetle. And it looks like that rare one!'

Luke put the beetle into my hands and we ran back to the village.

CHAPTER 7

Photos for the Magazine

When we got back, Mum was sitting on a blanket in the village square with a group of women around her. They were laughing and taking turns to pose in front of her camera.

'Mum, guess what?' I cried.

Mum turned. 'Hi David!'

'I have a surprise for you.' I opened my hand. 'I think it's that rhinoceros beetle. The one you've been looking for. Luke took me to a place in the jungle. There are lots of them. It's only just down the hill. We could easily carry you...'

Mum reached for the beetle and I saw tears in the corners of her eyes.

'Thank you, David. It's a beautiful beetle. It's the best gift...'

'But it isn't *the one*, is it?' I said.

'It's *like* the one we've been searching for. It's the same bright colour...'

'Is it rare?'

Mum wrinkled her nose, 'Well...'

'So, it's common then?'

'I wouldn't call it common!' She reached out her hand. 'Can I take a photo of you and Luke holding it?'

I hesitated. Mum knew I hated having my photo taken.

'Please.'

How could I say no? Luke stood beside me. Then the village women decided to crowd around too.'

'Great,' Mum called. 'Smile.'

She took a few shots, then leaned back exhausted. I felt tired too.

'I'd really hoped it was the rare beetle,' I muttered quietly to Mum. 'Then you could still have taken photos for the magazine.'

'That's just it,' Mum cried, sitting forward with a fresh burst of energy. 'I didn't have a chance to tell you. There's a wedding ceremony this afternoon. The women have been practising for the sing-sing and I've taken some fantastic shots of them dancing. The magazine will love them!'

I looked at the women decorated in their feathers and beads and shells. They looked so exotic with the lush, misty mountains as a backdrop.

'Then the trip hasn't been wasted?'

'Not at all. The photos will be great. I just hope the weather doesn't clear until after the ceremony!'

Mum's wish was granted. We stayed one more night and Mum was able to fill her backpack with rolls of film ready to be developed at home.

Luke and his family sat on the airstrip with us as we waited. We heard the rumble of an engine edging nearer. Then it was time to say goodbye.

I took a deep breath as we stepped into the tiny aeroplane. Luke waved and said he'd be waiting for my first letter. We'd decided to write to each other. I hadn't told him that I also planned to send a box of books and pens and some toys to the village school.

As I helped Mum into her seat, she squeezed my hand. 'Are you glad you came?' Mum asked.

The aeroplane was rolling down the runway. We picked up speed, hit the bump at the end of the airstrip and the plane bounced into the air.

'Yeehah!' I squealed.

Then I turned back to Mum and grinned. 'Very glad!' I said. 'It's been the best mother-and-son-time ever!'